THE CRUEL
SOLSTICE
by Sidney Keyes

ROUTLEDGE   LONDON

1943

TO

John Heath Stubbs

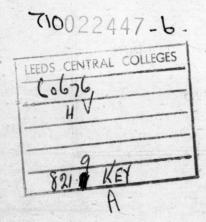

CONTENTS

Note. I have to thank the following for permission to reprint some of these poems: *Kingdom Come, The Listener, Modern Reading* and *Bugle Blast* (Messrs. Ivor Nicholson & Watson), *Poetry* (London), *Poetry Folios, Poetry Quarterly*, Messrs. Faber & Faber; and The Hogarth Press.

Though not precisely a sequence, the poems have been arranged in a rough order of thought; and should be read consecutively, with the section of *Legends* as a sort of interlude.

S. K.

LANDSCAPES AND FIGURES

Four Postures of Death

I. *DEATH AND THE MAIDEN*

He said, "Dance for me", and he said,
"You are too beautiful for the wind
To pick at, or the sun to burn". He said,
"I'm a poor tattered thing, but not unkind
To the sad dancer and the dancing dead".

So I smiled and a slow measure
Mastered my feet and I was happy then.
He said, "My people are gentle as lilies
And in my house there are no men
To wring your young heart with a foolish pleasure".

Because my boy had crossed me in a strange bed
I danced for him and was not afraid.
He said, "You are too beautiful for any man
To finger; you shall stay a maid
For ever in my kingdom and be comforted".

He said, "You shall be my daughter and your feet move
In finer dances, maiden; and the hollow
Halls of my house shall flourish with your singing".
He beckoned and I knew that I must follow
Into the kingdom of no love.

II. *DEATH AND THE LOVERS*

The Lover: *The briars fumble with the moon;*
Far have I come, O far away
And heartsick sore, my own sweeting.

The Woman: *I stand before the ordered prison room.*
I can give you no lover's greeting.

The Lover: *Wind cracks the clouds, so has my face cracked open*
With longing all this while, my cold face turning
Hopelessly to you, like a hound's blind muzzle
Turned to the moon.

The Woman: *O you bring in a sickly moon*
And you bring in the rain:
I will not open, my true love is gone,
You are his ghost. O never come again.

The Lover: *My feet are bleeding, you called me and your face*
Called me a daylong dreary journeying.

The Woman: *Get back, get back into your likely place.*
The time is past for all this havering.

The Lover: *I am a poor boy, pity*
A poor boy on the roads, after your love.

The Woman: *It is too late: seek out a storied city*
To house your silliness. Oh, my lost love . . .

Death: *Is here behind you. Get you in*
Out of that muscular salacious wind.
Lie down by me: I have an art
To comfort you and still your restless mind.

The Woman: *I'll close the window; and God send*
We are damned easily . . .

Death: *Lie down by me, be gentle: at the end*
Of time, God's quiet hands will kill your fantasy.

The Lover: *And strangle me, God's horny fingers, huge*
Fingers of broken cloud, great creaking hands
That so beset me; briar-nails tear free
My soul into your wisdom, ravish me
Since she will not . . .

The Woman: *I am afraid, your hands are strong and cold.*
Are you my enemy, or my forsaken lover?

Death: *Lie soft, lie still. I am sleep's cruel brother.*

III. DEATH AND THE LADY

O quietly I wait by the window and my frayed fine hand
Rests in the autumn sunlight.
                                    Quietly
The garden trees shake down their crown of leaves.
I have no fear because I have no lover.

I was never acquisitive, never would bind
Any man for myself: so from this brown and golden
Season of loneliness let him call me softly—
Expecting my compliance, not my welcome.

It may be an hour's play, this waiting for the word—
He will speak softly, for they all spoke softly—
Or I may fill an autumn with contrition
And waiting for the arm across my shoulders.

Yet he must use no lover's talk to me,
Nor shall his hand be ringed, even with sapphires.
He need not dance, for I have danced with others.
O let him come as bare and white as winter.

The wind comes and goes. The leaves and clouds
Fall through the branches. In a dream
Or perhaps a picture, quite without surprise
I turn to meet the question in his eyes.

IV. DEATH AND THE PLOWMAN

The Rider: O don't, don't ever ask me for alms:
               The winter way I'm riding. Beggar, shun
               My jingling bonebag equipage, beware
               My horse's lifted hoof, the sinewed whip.
               I am the man started a long time since
               To drive into the famous land some call
               Posterity, some famine, some the valley
               Of bones, valley of bones, valley of dry
               Bones where a critical wind is always searching
               The poor dried marrow for a drop of truth.
               Better for you to ask no alms, my friend.

The Plowman: It's only the wind holds my poor bones together,
               So take me with you to that famous land.
               There I might wither, as I'm told some do,
               Out of my rags and boast at last
               The integrated skeleton of truth.

The Rider: The wind creeps sharper there, my hopeful friend,
               Than you imagine. There the crooked trees
               Bend like old fingers; and at Hallowmass
               The Lord calls erring bones to dance a figure.

The Plowman: What figure, friend? Why should I fear that dancing?

The Rider: No man may reasonably dance
               That figure, friend.   One saw it, one Ezekiel
               Was only spared to tell of it. That valley
               Is no man's proper goal, but some must seek it.

The Plowman: *I might get clothing there. A skeleton*
Cannot go naked.

The Rider: *Naked as the sky*
And lonely as the elements, the man
Who knows that land. The drypoint artist there
Scrabbles among the wreckage; poets follow
The hard crevasses, silly as starved gulls
That scream behind the plow. Don't stop me, friend,
Unless you are of those, and your fool's pride
Would lure you to that land. . . .

The Plowman: *I will go with you.*
Better plow-following, the searching wind
About my bones than this nonentity.

The Rider: *Then get you up beside me, gull-brained fool.*

Both: *We're driving to the famous land some call*
Posterity, some famine, some the valley
Of bones, valley of bones, valley of dry
Bones where there is no heat nor hope nor dwelling:
But cold security, the one and only
Right of a workless man without a home.

Cervières

Look, Aimée, and you, Victor, look—
The birds have taken all our cherries—
Down in the brown-walled orchard on the hillside
The cherry-trees are weeping for their fruit;
Only the clusters of green stalks
Remain; the stones are scattered on the grass.
There will be no more cherries, not this summer
Nor next, if we get another. God!
It's beyond bearing that they eat our cherries

And fly away and leave the trees in mourning.
Soon an invader will be taking more than cherries:
They'll be stealing our dreams or breaking up
Our history for firewood.

Children, see
The avenues of cherry-trees are broken
And trampled boughs crawl in the dust. See, Victor,
How the sun bouncing off the mountain strikes
Christ's wooden throat above the cemetery:
Flesh broken like our cherry-trees and ravished.
The path runs open and smiling down the hill;
It leaps the walls and hides behind the ruins.

Now take this moment and create its image
Impregnable to time or trespasser,
And turn your mind to realise your loss.
The cherry-trees are broken and their fruit
Sown on the indecipherable mountains.
Realise your loss and take it in your hands
And turn it like a pebble. You perceive
It has a stone's dumb smell; its patterns
Plot some forgotten map. Regard your loss.

Planting this lump of pain, perhaps a flower
Might burst from it; perhaps a cherry-tree,
Perhaps a world or a new race of men.

Regard your loss. The blossoms of the cherry
Are rotten now; the branch is violated;
The fruit is stolen and our dreams have failed.
Yet somewhere—O beyond what bitter ranges?—
A seed drops from the sky and like a bomb
Explodes into our orchard's progeny,
And so our care may colonise a desert.

14

They cannot break our trees or waste our dreams,
For their despoiling is a kind of sowing.

Aimée and Victor, stop crying. Can't you understand
They cannot steal our cherries or our joy?
Let them take what they want, even our dreams.
Somewhere our loss will plant a better orchard.

Advice for a Journey

The drums mutter for war and soon we must begin
To seek the country where they say that joy
Springs flowerlike among the rocks, to win
The fabulous golden mountain of our peace.

O my friends, we are too young
For explorers, have no skill nor compass,
Nor even that iron certitude which swung
Our fathers at their self-fulfilling North.

So take no rations, remember not your homes—
Only the blind and stubborn hope to track
This wilderness. The thoughtful leave their bones
In windy foodless meadows of despair.

Never look back, nor too far forward search
For the white Everest of your desire;
The screes roll underfoot and you will never reach
Those brittle peaks which only clouds may walk.

Others have come before you. The immortal
Live like reflections and their frozen faces
Will give you courage to ignore the subtle
Sneer of the gentian and the iceworn pebble.

The fifes cry death and the sharp winds call.
Set your face to the rock; go on, go out
Into the bad lands of battle, into the cloud-wall
Of the future, my friends, and leave your fear.

Go forth, my friends, the raven is no sibyl;
Break the clouds' anger with your unchanged faces.
You'll find, maybe, the dream under the hill—
But never Canaan, nor any golden mountain.

Epithalamium
for R. B. and H. S., October '42

O you will have no bells and the winter is coming,
But now the corn lies down to the stumbling thresher,
The sycamore drops its yellow-winged projectiles
And winter is coming, but first the season of fruit.

Your bells will be the voices of autumn rivers,
Your wine will be the dew on the fallen apple:
I sing for you who at the end of summer
Have crowned the year and come together at last.

There's so much burning in the autumn world.
The flames spread through the stubble, and the wind
Comes out of Russia with a smell of fire.
The reapers do not sing, but the sickle whispers
Among the leaning wheat in the heat of noon.

O you have seen, as I have seen, the folly
Of those who think lost time can be repaid:
The girl who, mad with sorrow, hung her ring
On the wind's finger, was not half so vain.

I sing for you who at the end of summer
Have crowned the year and come together at last.

These nights are kind as the memory of a mother.
The geese track south across the heavy moon.
Your winter will be a triumph of clear decision
And what incredible spring may lie beyond?
O live and love to see your happy children
Deny the sorrow of a burning world.

Though you will have no bells and the winter is coming
I sing your courage, who expect the spring.

Moonlight Night on the Port

Some were unlucky. Blown a mile to shoreward
Their crossed hands lie among the bitter marsh-grass.

Link arms and sing. The moon sails out
Spreading distraction on the faces, drawing
The useful hands to birdclaws. . . .
                                        If a ring
Flashes, what matter? Other hands are ringless.
We'll never go home to-night, never to-night.

And some shall be pulled down, revolving sickly
On the tide's whim, their bare feet scraping sand.

The moon is out, my lady; lady of different
Voices and gestures, with the same cold eyes.
The buoy swings ringing. Under the curved seawall
My hands reveal your soundings all the same.

Some were more gallant, dragged across the seabed
In iron cages, coughing out their lungs.

Singing in bars, running before the seven
Set winds of the heart; bearing our weakness bravely
Through all the frigid seasons, we have weighed
The chances against us, and refuse no kisses—
Even the tide's kiss on this dog-toothed shore.

For some are lucky, leaving their curved faces
Propped in the moonlight while their bodies drown.

Two Offices of a Sentry

I. OFFICE FOR NOON

At the field's border, where the cricket chafes
His brittle wings among the yellow weed,
I pause to hear the sea unendingly sifted
Between the granite fingers of the cape.
At this twelfth hour of unrelenting summer
I think of those whose ready mouths are stopped.
I remember those who crouch in narrow graves.
I weep for those whose eyes are full of sand.

II. OFFICE FOR MIDNIGHT

The ones who gave themselves to every moment
Till time grew gentle as a sated lover;
The young swift-footed and the old keen-eyed,
Whose roads are freedom and whose stars are constant,
Stand by me as I watch this empty town.

I am in love with the wildness of the living.
I am in love with the rhythms of dead limbs.
I am in love with all those who have entered
The night that smells of petals and of dust.

Seascape

For R. J.

Our country was a country drowned long since,
By shark-toothed currents drowned:
And in that country walk the generations,
The dancing generations with grey eyes
Whose touch would be like rain, the generations
Who never thought to justify their beauty.
There once the flowering cherry grasped the wall
With childish fingers, once the gull swung crying
Across the morning or the evening mist;
Once high heels rattled on the terrace
Over the water's talk, and the wind lifted
The hard leaves of the bay; the white sand drifted
Under the worm-bored rampart, under the white eyelid.

Our country was a country washed with colour.
Its light was good to us, sharp limning
The lover's secret smile, the fine-drawn fingers;
It drew long stripes between the pointed jaws
Of sea-bleached wreckage grinning through the wrack
And turned cornelian the flashing eyeball.
For here the tide sang like a riding hero
Across the rock-waste, and the early sun
Was shattered in the teeth of shuttered windows.

But now we are the gowned lamenters
Who stand among the junipers and ruins.
We are the lovers who defied the sea
Until the tide returning threw us up
A foreign corpse with blue-rimmed eyes, and limbs
Drawn limp and racked between the jigging waves.

Greenwich Observatory

This onion-dome holds all intricacies
Of intellect and star-struck wisdom; so
Like Coleridge's head with multitudinous
Passages riddled, full of strange instruments
Unbalanced by a touch, this organism
From wires and dials spins introverted life.
It never looks, squat on its concrete shoulders
Down at the river's swarming life, nor sees
Cranes' groping insect-like activity
Nor slow procession of funnels past the docks.
Turning its inner wheels, absorbed in problems
Of space and time, it never hears
Birds singing in the park or children's laughter.
Alive, but in another way, it broods
On this its Highgate, hypnotised
In lunar reverie and calculation.
Yet night awakes it; blind lids open
Leaden to look upon the moon:
A single goggling telescopic eye
Enfolds the spheric wonder of the sky.

Paul Klee

The short-faced goblins with their heavy feet
Trampled your dreams, their spatulate
Fingers have torn the tracery of your wisdom:
But childlike you would not cry out, transforming
Your enemies to little angry phantoms
In clarity of vision exorcised.
Until at last they conquered by attrition,
And draining the last dregs of love away,
They left you from the angular
Prison of primary fears no way but flight:
Yet never could invade your waterworld of spirit
Since half divining there among the dance
Of shadowed currents lurking ever
Their unguessed image, luminous with fear.
And so they stirred the shallows till the sky
Flew blue in shards and thought sank even deeper,
Where crouched your passion's residue confined:
The evil centre of a child's clear mind.

War Poet

I am the man who looked for peace and found
My own eyes barbed.
I am the man who groped for words and found
An arrow in my hand.
I am the builder whose firm walls surround
A slipping land.
When I grow sick or mad
Mock me not nor chain me:
When I reach for the wind
Cast me not down:
Though my face is a burnt book
And a wasted town.

William Yeats in Limbo

Where folds the central lotus
Flesh and soul could never seek?
Under what black-scar'd mountain
May Pallas with Adonis meet?

Spirit-bodies' loveliness
Cannot expiate my pain:
How should I learn wisdom
Being old and profane?

My thoughts have swarmed like bees
In an old ruined tower:
How should I go to drive them out
Lacking joy and power?

How could I learn youth again,
With figured symbols weaving
Truth so easily, now I
Am old and unbelieving?

By what chicanery of time
May sword and sheath be separated?
Silent be the singer who thinks of me
And how I was defeated.

Remember Your Lovers

Young men walking the open streets
Of death's republic, remember your lovers.

When you foresaw with vision prescient
The planet pain rising across your sky

We fused your sight in our soft burning beauty:
We laid you down in meadows drunk with cowslips
And led you in the ways of our bright city.
Young men who wander death's vague meadows,
Remember your lovers who gave you more than flowers.

When truth came prying like a surgeon's knife
Among the delicate movements of your brain
We called your spirit from its narrow den
And kissed your courage back to meet the blade—
Our anæsthetic beauty saved you then.
Young men whose sickness death has cured at last,
Remember your lovers and covet their disease.

When you woke grave-chilled at midnight
To pace the pavement of your bitter dream
We brought you back to bed and brought you home
From the dark antechamber of desire
Into our lust as warm as candle-flame.
Young men who lie in the carven beds of death,
Remember your lovers who gave you more than dreams.

From the sun sheltering your careless head
Or from the painted devil your quick eye,
We led you out of terror tenderly
And fooled you into peace with our soft words
And gave you all we had and let you die.
Young men drunk with death's unquenchable wisdom,
Remember your lovers who gave you more than love.

The Gardener

If you will come on such a day
As this, between the pink and yellow lines
Of parrot-tulips, I will be your lover.
My boots flash as they beat the silly gravel.
O come, this is your day.

Were you to lay your hand like a veined leaf
Upon my square-cut hand, I would caress
The shape of it, and that would be enough.
I note the greenfly working on the rose.
Time slips between my fingers like a leaf.

Do you resemble the silent pale-eyed angels
That follow children? Is your face a flower?
The lovers and the beggars leave the park—
And still you will not come. The gates are closing.

O it is terrible to dream of angels.

St. John Baptist

I, John, not reed but root;
Not vested priest nor saviour but a voice
Crying daylong like a cricket in the heat,
Demand your worship. Not of me
But of the traveller I am calling
From beyond Jordan and the limestone hills,
Whose runner and rude servant I am only.
Not man entirely but God's watchman,
I dwell among these blistered rocks
Awaiting the wide dawn, the wonder
Of His first coming and the Dove's descent.

24

Night Estuary

And yet the spiked moon menacing
The great humped dykes, scaring the plaintive seafowl,
Makes no right image, wakes no assertive echo.
Though one may stride the dykes with face upturned
To the yellow inflammation in the sky
And nostrils full of the living samphire scent,
There is no kindness in man's heart for these.
In this place, and at this unmeaning hour,
There is no home for a man's hope or his sorrow.

O you lion-hearted poet's griefs, or griefs
Wild as the curlew's cry of passage;
O hope uneasy as the rising ebb
Among the sedges, cold and questing guest;
Leave me alone this hour with the restive night.
Allow me to accept the witless landscape.

William Byrd

I have come very far, Lord. In my time
Men's mouths have been shut up, the gabble and whine
Of shot has drowned the singing. You will pardon
My praise that rises only from a book—
(How long shall that book be hidden
Under a scarecrow gown, under evil writings?)
And you will pardon the tricks, the secret rooms,
The boarded windows, your house again a stall.
These things have made my house of praise more holy.
And so I try to remember how it was

When lovers sang like finches, and the Word
Was music.
                    Lord, I am no coward,
But an old man remembering the candle-flames
Reflected in the scroll-work, frozen trees
Praying for Advent, the willow cut at Easter.
The quires are dumb. My spirit sings in silence.
You will appoint the day of my arising.

Early Spring

Now that the young buds are tipped with a falling sun—
Each twig a candle, a martyr, St. Julian's branched stag—
And the shadows are walking the cobbled square like soldiers
With their long legs creaking and their pointed hands
Reaching the railings and fingering the stones
Of what expended, unprojected graves:
The soil's a flirt, the lion Time is tamed,
And pain like a cat will come home to share your room.

Hopes for a Lover

I'd have you proud as red brocade
And such a sight as Venus made
Extravagantly stepping from a shell.

I'd have you clear your way before
With such a look as Aias wore
On his way back from hell.

I'd have you strong as spider's strand
And all volcanic as the land
Where the nymph fooled that cunning Ulysses.

I'd have you arrogantly ride
Love's flurry, as the turning seas
Bore Arion upon a fish.
My last and dearest wish—
That you should let the arrows of my pride
Come at you again and again and never touch you.

North Sea

The evening thickens. Figures like a frieze
Cross the sea's face, their cold unlifted heads
Disdainful of the wind that pulls their hair.
The brown light lies along the harbour wall.

And eastward looking, eastward wondering
I meet the eyes of Heine's ghost, who saw
His failure in the grey forsaken waves
At Rulenstein one autumn. And between
Rises the shape in more than memory
Of Düsseldorf, the ringing, river-enfolding
City that brought such sorrow on us both.

A Hope for Those Separated by War

They crossed her face with blood,
They hung her heart.
They dragged her through a pit
Full of quick sorrow.
Yet her small feet
Ran back on the morrow.

They took his book and caged
His mind in a dark house.
They took his bright eyes
To light their rooms of doubt.
Yet his thin hands
Crawled back and found her out.

Song: The Heart's Assurance

O never trust the heart's assurance—
Trust only the heart's fear:
And what I'm saying is, Go back, my lovely—
Though you will never hear.

O never trust your pride of movement—
Trust only pride's distress:
The only holy limbs are the broken fingers
Still raised to praise and bless.

For the careless heart is bound with chains
And terribly cast down:
The beast of pride is hunted out
And baited through the town.

Design for a Monument

The stone doves settle on the lady's tomb.

Grey scrolls of lettering upon her eyes
Will never hide the image of regret;
And she who walked in a rich robe of safety
Now shrinks beneath the rough immodest shroud.

O elegies are empty as the waiting
Of timid ancestors and scraping parents
Who worked so long towards that ruined face.
All walks at evening among the stolid yews,
And mornings at high windows, are forgotten
Like folds in a gold robe laid out to rot.
The lovers who rode with her lie scattered
Among their horses' big-eyed skulls in the meadow;
The yellow charlock scratches at her door.

It is not easy to lament a lady
Whose past was greater than the singer's age.
They who fly falcons at the angry sun
Or ride black horses through the armoured night
Have wept for her a day, then fallen sick
And laid their bones in cold heraldic houses:
And I am left to pause before her tomb
Where grey doves cover her with granite leaves.

The Cruel Solstice

To-night the stranger city and the old
Moon that stands over it proclaim
A cruel solstice, coming ice and cold
Thoughts and the darkening of the heart's flame.

"Stand up", speaks soul, "let wisdom turn the time
Into an image of your day's despite";
O clever soul, we were born separate,
Held only in hard glance or studied rhyme.

"Sleep then, tired singer, stop the mouth
Of the unhappy month and take your rest."
O cunning voice, I have not strength enough,
Being no stranger here, but uncouth guest.

So must I walk or falter by the wall
Wondering at my impotence
Of thought and action; at the fall
Of love and cities and the heart's false diligence.

To-night I cannot speak, remembering
For all my daily talk, I dare not enter
The empty month; can only stand and think
Of you, my dearest, and the approaching winter.

A Renunciation

Strong angels bear God's canopy,
Strong horsemen ride the loose immoderate wind:
But O my dark girl from her balcony
Laughs down and puts their glory out of mind.

Sharp stars are wiser than the astronomer,
The stinking goat more potent than the great
Lover of girls, that cold Casanova:
And righteous wars forget the cause of hate.

The high djinn-master Solomon
Could never understand his women's talk:
So I would be an unobservant man
Frequenting gardens where dark women walk.

Lover's Complaint

I. NOCTURNE

The trains cry and are frightened
Far from my distraction; spare
My peace, my voice, my city
Of desolation, desolate because you are there.

There was a month and two people walked in it
But were not you or I:
My sight is broken and the signs are taken
That kept me safe in abject poetry.

Spare too my willing mind
That served your images:
There is a night and two people lie in it,
And the green planet rages.

Were I to pass now on the creaking stair
You would not know my face:
The months and the night and my own mind
Have taken a ghost's grace.

For my private streets and summers
Are any alien comer's;
And the tall miraculous city
That I walked in will never house me.

II. AUBADE

O sing, caged lark, sing caged
Poetical bird, you liar;
Sing high to-day, your female
Rapture, your cagebird fire
Won't fool me now, the day's already aged
Ten years and your voice falls stale.

O sing, erotic season, sing
Dream-heavy mind;
Light's terrible ministry
Perform, clear morning wind.
But my ears have aged and everything
Has turned round wretchedly.

Lament for Harpsichord: The Flowering Orchards

The days and faces: O to take the faces
And crumbling features of my love and build them
Into a wall about our flowered April.
Rain seeks the root. The cloudy spring approaches.

If we could for a moment be alone,
Had it been possible for us to meet
Among the flowering orchards of the South
Or when the summer flashed and rocketed
Between green sedges like a kingfisher:
If we could be alone, my dear, my dearest,
With the pale light of April and the open
Roads of a tired heart, my far, my farthest,
There might be hope and heavy trees this summer
Instead of these hard blooms, this backward spring—
The gapped walls and the falling faces,
The scraggy birds that will not learn to sing.

Those flowering orchards, O to save those orchards
Of starred illusion from the climbing blight.
Silver it settles on the leaves and fissures
The strong bole slowly, to its circled heart.
If we could be alone for a moment only
While the spring grows, while blossoms fight
Within the bud. . . .
                    If we had met before
And in another place, what wonders might we see
Sheltered by days and faces, under a flowering tree?

The Migrant

Slimmer than thrush, the ringneck ousel
Haunts these black becks, recalling chalk-ribbed downs
You walk this month; the heavy wrack
Stumbling across them in the winter dusk;
The gulls' extended shadows on the turf;
A Hampshire naturalist seeking, noting

33

The flocks, the fluting birds, (was it indeed
Migration brought them, or mere Providence?)
The ringnecked birds in autumn on those downs.
So by the millrace and the stony ridge
I look for something different, for a sign
That love has flown into another country,
Migrating from this frost—not, as I fear,
Frozen and starved. The quick bird calls
Thinly among the willows, and I think
Of spring and of that winter friend. O voice,
O bird-throat, bird-throat, you know not
My deeper fear of time, my silly hope
That spring may find us eager and unchanged.

The Doubtful Season

The doubtful season of the brain's black weather
Blew through me, but you waited for its end.
My months were all named backwards till you showed me
That even the mind is not deceived for ever.

O in October it would be the blazoned
Leaves of the chestnut on the cobbled pavement:
And we would seek in the corridors of autumn
Denial of faith and of the summer's achievement.

And in the early year it was another
Sign of evasion when the poplars clattered
To sharpened ears above the metal river—
And I would turn to find your eyes were shuttered.

Even that almost parting on the stair
I could not understand, nor why the candles

34

Sprouted such flowers between our sculptured faces:
Nor why the river glinted in your hair.

O in July it was our love was started
Like any hare among the watchful grasses;
Its running is my song, my only story
How time turns back and the doubtful season passes.

The Promised Landscape

For R. J.

How shall I sing for you—
Sharing only
The scared dream of a soldier:
A young man's unbearable
Dream of possession?
How shall I sing for you
With the foul tongue of a soldier?

We march through new mountains
Where crows inhabit
The pitiful cairns.
At morning, the rock-pools
Are matted with ice.
But you are the mountains
And you the journey.

We lie in a ruined farm
Where rats perform
Marvels of balance
Among the rafters.

35

And rain kisses my lips
Because you are the sky
That bends always over me.

How shall I sing for you
Knowing only
The explorer's sorrow,
The soldier's weariness?
New ranges and rivers
Are never quite revealing
Your promised figure.

How dare I sing for you
I the least worthy
Of lovers you've had:
You the most lovely
Of possible landscapes?

September, 1942

The Kestrels

When I would think of you, my mind holds only
The small defiant kestrels—how they cut
The raincloud with sharp wings, continually circling
About a storm-rocked elm, with passionate cries.
It was an early month. The plow cut hard.
The may was knobbed with chilly buds. My folly
Was great enough to lull away my pride.

There is no virtue now in blind reliance
On place or person or the forms of love.
The storm bears down the pivotal tree, the cloud

36

Turns to the net of an inhuman fowler
And drags us from the air. Our wings are clipped.
Yet still our love and luck lies in our parting:
Those cries and wings surprise our surest act.

Medallion

Bull-chested and iron-eyed heroes
And weeping women
Surround me while I sleep;
Waking, I meet the continual procession
Of hawk-headed, bird-clawed women
And weeping men.

The Glass Tower in Galway

I

One was an eye and others
Snake-headed travesties; one high-legged and mincing
As a stork. And there were whining small ones
Like sickly children. O they were a beastly
Sea-born race, spawned on the rocks of Galway
Among the dried shark-eggs and the dirty froth.
They moved and cried and the wind blew hard from the West,
Ruffling the treacherous pale places over the reefs.
They cried, "Ours is the land",
And the gulls dared not dispute them
Nor even the old falcon circling the misty cape.
They took the crooked fields and straggling coasts
Of Galway, spreading later East and South
Through heather-topped hills and the stinking bogs of Connaught,
To caper lastly on the inland pastures
Where only the moon and the waving grasses mocked them.
But where the sea had retched them up
They built a tower, above the cross-grained tides
And wheezing potholed beaches, on a headland;
Of glass they reared it, riveted askew,
Sustained by witchcraft; in the autumn gales
Ringing like a goblet till the mountains quivered.
It was their shrine, and cruel sea-rites
Went forward there while they possessed the land:
Sometimes it shook with screaming and children's corpses

Drifted southward, mauled by the grumbling seals.
Yet still on summer nights impassively
It faced the empty West with its inane transparency.

II

But as the inhuman years neared their completion
A race came from the South; sun-bronzed
Cloud-riding Danaan people out of Egypt.
And there were battles. First among the ravaged
Hills and then raging by the stony beaches.
Wars passed; the sea took many dead, the tower
Fell and its rites were celebrated
Now only in the deep sea caverns where its masters
Sought refuge; now the fretful tide
Coughed round those altars without sacrifice;
Outlawed by history, the sea-born race
Rotted off Galway, the Atlantic shark
And groping spider-crab their only heir.
Those reefs and beaches now lay shadowless
Under the moon; the wheeling falcon saw
A new age coming, like the early sun
Gilding the spindrift, bronze on the wet sand.

III

But even that age is dead and songs
Forget its buried kings who lie
Under high cairns, their requiem the curlews'
Insatiable crying, their epitaph
In lichens written, and great deeds engraved
On buried shards of bronze. For history
Despises even them, turning their prowess
Into a tale of ogres, fame and truth
Lost in the wreck of their enormous bones.

IV

Bats roost in the high white halls
And the heroes are finished.

Their swords are stacked for scrap
In the cold waste places.

Their tombs scattered and broken
Nourish the blue thistle.

For time will never repent
Nor the seasons pity them.

There's no hope in hoping now:
God has left us like a girl.

The Bards

Now it is time to remember the winter festivals
Of the old world, and see their raftered halls
Hung with hard holly; tongues' confusion; slow
Beat of the heated blood in those great palaces
Decked with the pale and sickled mistletoe;
And voices dying when the blind bard rises
Robed in his servitude, and the high harp
Of sorrow sounding, stills those upturned faces.

O it is such long learning, loneliness
And dark despite to master
The bard's blind craft; in bitterness
Of heart to strike the strings and muster
The shards of pain to harmony, not sharp
With anger to insult the merry guest.

O it is glory for the old man singing
Dead valour and his own days coldly cursed.

How ten men fell by one heroic sword
And of fierce foray by the unwatched ford,
Sing, blinded face; quick hands in darkness groping
Pluck the sad harp; sad heart forever hoping
Valhalla may be songless, enter
The moment of your glory, out of clamour
Moulding your vision to such harmony
That drunken heroes cannot choose but honour
Your stubborn blinded pride, your inward winter.

Simon Magus

The hands affright, it is the cunning hands
Have driven my weak masters out of doors:
For a gold piece or healing water-kiss
Shaped like a cross, make my hands strong as yours.

The hand fails because of the unpurged eye.
The kiss fails because of the cold coin.
There is no power on earth can circumvent
The stubborn intellect, proud as a god's pain.

Go pray, Simon; hide your noisy heart
Clapper-tongued and lolling with conceit.
Meet your master in his house of fire
And practise wonders on the silly dead.
For you the mathematics of desire,
The frigid neophyte, the cold symbolic bed.

Don Juan in Winter

Where once it was under archways
The legendary two-backed beast and bright
As younger years the moonlight, dog-legged shadows
Hunting not then, sparing your hopeful night:

Now they run loose about the traitor streets,
You see in archways waiting the wronged man
You spitted, and the beast run down and cornered
Can only howl, harder its hunting than

The shame and terror of its own past quarry,
The cry at midnight. Now the hunt is up
For every dealer in expensive passion
And every drinker from the jewelled cup.

Alone in winter now, you dare not loiter
Along old ways, beside the terraced shore:
Your steps avoid the high-wrought palaces
Whose keys your fingers were, but are no more.

It is not vengefully nor yet in wisdom
You're punished so. The night will never fail;
But pretty faces fall and fail and never
Escape from their tired mirrors. Years as pale

As shipwreck are your portion, you once diver;
Once hunter, hunting. Serenaded windows yawn
Satirically like old gap-toothed women,
And age's dunghill cock crows up your dawn.

Glaucus

The various voices are his poem now.

Under the currents, under the shifting lights
Of midway water, rolls his fleshy wreck:
Its gurnard eye reflects those airy heights
Where once it noted white Arcturus set.

Gull-swift and swerving, the wet spirit freed
Skims the huge breakers. Watching at the prow
Of any southbound vessel, sailor, heed
Never that petrel spirit, cruel as pride.

Let no cliff-haunting woman, no girl claim
Kinship with Glaucus, neither sow
The tide with daffodils, nor call his name
Into the wind, for he is glorified—
And cold Aegean voices speak his fame.

Dido's Lament for Aeneas

He never loved the frenzy of the sun
Nor the clear seas.
He came with hero's arms and bullock's eyes
Afraid of nothing but his nagging gods.
He never loved the hollow-sounding beaches
Nor rested easily in carven beds.

The smoke blows over the breakers, the high pyre waits.
His mind was a blank wall throwing echoes,
Not half so subtle as the coiling flames.
He never loved my wild eyes nor the pigeons
Inhabiting my gates.

43

Rome Remember

The bright waves scour the wound of Carthage.
The shadows of gulls run spiderlike through Carthage.
The cohorts of the sand are wearing Carthage
Hollow and desolate as a turning wave;
But the bronze eagle has flown east from Rome.

Rome remember, remember the seafowls' sermon
That followed the beaked ships westward to their triumph.
O Rome, you city of soldiers, remember the singers
That cry with dead voices along the African shore.

Rome remember, the courts of learning are tiled
With figures from the east like running nooses.
The desolate bodies of boys in the blue glare
Of falling torches cannot stir your passion.
Remember the Greeks who measured out your doom.
Remember the soft funereal Etruscans.

O when the rain beats with a sound like bells
Upon your bronze-faced monuments, remember
This European fretful-fingered rain
Will turn to swords in the hand of Europe's anger.
Remember the Nordic snarl and the African sorrow.

The bronze wolf howls when the moon turns red.
The trolls are massing for their last assault.
Your dreams are full of claws and scaly faces
And the Gothic arrow is pointed at your heart.

Rome remember your birth in Trojan chaos.
O think how savage will be your last lamenters:
How alien the lovers of your ghost.

Lament for Adonis

I bring you branches and sing scattering branches.
My feet have never turned this way before.
My tears are statues in my lighted eyes.
My mind is a stone with grief going over it
Like white brook-water in the early year.
I bring you tears and sing scattering tears.
My grief for you is cold and heavy as iron.
Your beauty was a wound in the world's side.

I bring you blood and sing scattering blood.

Little Drawda

All Souls, '41

Under the shaken trees, wait O unlucky
Returner, you rejected one:
There is no way of comforting you. Wait
Under the shaken trees and the clock striking one.

In the moon's wicked glitter linger now
You tired ghost:
You have no stance of safety but shift
In the moon's glitter, an uprooted ghost.

On this strong night, remain you lonely
Seeker beside me, though my heart is dumb:
We may together solve the unexpected
Secret of living, now that the clock is dumb.

Timoshenko

Hour ten he rose, ten-sworded, every finger
A weighted blade, and strapping round his loins
The courage of attack, he threw the window
Open to look on his appointed night.

Where lay, beneath the winds and creaking flares
Tangled like lovers or alone assuming
The wanton postures of the drunk with sleep,
An army of twisted limbs and hollow faces
Thrown to and fro between the winds and shadows.
O hear the wind, the wind that shakes the dawn.
And there before the night, he was aware
Of the flayed fields of home, and black with ruin
The helpful earth under the tracks of tanks.
His bladed hand, in pity falling, mimicked
The crumpled hand lamenting the broken plow;
And the oracular metal lips in anger
Squared to the shape of the raped girl's yelling mouth.
He heard the wind explaining nature's sorrow
And humming in the wire hair of the dead.

He turned, and his great shadow on the wall
Swayed like a tree. His eyes grew cold as lead.
Then, in a rage of love and grief and pity
He made the pencilled map alive with war.

Orestes and the Furies

This self-absorbed Orestes speaking riddles
Wanders the falling woods of his own past;
Remembering the pillared house, he weeps for
A mother murdered and a sister lost.

Of Agamemnon felled like groaning timber—
Alas the day he turned his back on Troy—
The hunted hero muses, and his mother
Who made him tremble like a lovestruck boy.

The mask of tragic pride upon his features
Is painted with inexorable art.
The guilty hands of mother and of sister
Are both the iron hand upon his heart.

Observing shapes of judgment in the sky
He seeks the dark, yet dare not turn his back
Upon those shattered mirrors where he sees
The snake-haired Furies running on his track.

Time Will Not Grant

Time will not grant the unlined page
Completion or the hand respite:
The Magi stray, the heavens rage,
The careful pilgrim stumbles in the night.

Take pen, take eye and etch
Your vision on this unpropitious time;
Faces are fluid, actions never reach
Perfection but in reflex or in rhyme.

Take now, not soon; your lost
Minutes roost home like curses.
Nicolo, Martin, every unhoused ghost
Proclaims time's strange reverses.

Fear was Donne's peace; to him,
Charted between the minstrel cherubim,
Terror was decent. Rilke tenderly
Accepted autumn like a rooted tree.
But I am frightened after every good day
That all my life must change and fall away.

Anarchy

Rising, the light ran round inside his eyes.
Then at a later hour, without surprise,
He noted singing birds that raked the sky
With pointed rods of sound like surgeons' knives.

The walls were scrawled with moss. The trees
Grabbed at the sun like grey anemones.
At noon he met a girl whose body sang
Thin as a cricket, till his eardrums rang.

Black dancers crossed his brain. The bearded sun
Whirled past him, locked with prancing Capricorn.
A dog began to howl, until he cried
It was too much. And then his wonder died.

Evening found him lost but unafraid
Surveying the wry landscape in his head.
Night ravished him, and so was brought to birth
A great cold passion to destroy the earth.

To Keep Off Fears

Fear of jammed window and of rising footsteps
Out of fear's stair, where a tall phantom mounts
Through time and action at the brain:

Fear of the enormous mountain leaning
Across thought's lake, where blinded fishes move
As cold and intricate as love:

Fear of the fisherman
Who raised Leviathan
On a steel line from his creative mirror:
Fear of the moonlight shifting against the door:

Fear finally of tripwire and garotte
Reaching possessive from an easy air:
These bring the careful man into despair.

Then let me never crouch against the wall
But meet my fears and fight them till I fall.

Being Not Proud

Being not proud to praise a lonely man's
Heroic loveless dream-humility most often
Comes to the drunken or the moonstruck mind—
I seek new pain to soften
Like rain the stony soul, or careful wind.

Moses' great parleying on Sinai
Brought anger on him and defeat:
Love, being no frigid stonecrop-flower,
Blooms not among pride's wrack and sleet
Nor ornaments an introverted tower.

The bones of heroes crowned with stone and statue
Nourish no flower nor bitter cry;
Yet groping painfully, love's roots may save
The dumb soul of a stone, or justify
The holed heart in a crossroad grave.

The Uncreated Images

The commerce of lithe limbs is fool's delight.

O hours and watches, O unending summer
Within the lover's blood and cloudy blooms
That nightly rise and break about the body—
These are the currency of dreams and language,
The uncreated images of truth.

Night's wink is momentary, and dividing
The coloured shapes of passion which it spawned,
Night strikes through the membrane to the gristled socket
And tumbles like a pebble through the skull.

There is no speech to tell the shape of love
Nor any but the wounded eye to see it;
Whether in memory, or listening to the talk
Of rain among the gutters; or at dawn
The sentry's feet striking the chilly yard,
There is no synonym for love's great word—
No way of comforting the limbs
That have lain lovelocked at an earlier season,
Nor any coin to close the tired eye
That day chastises with its rods of light.
The separate limbs perform a faithless task—
The eye devours created images.

The commerce of lithe limbs is fool's delight,
Cry limb and eyeball, waiting for the night.

Against Divination

Not in the night time, in the weary bed
Comes wisdom, neither to the wild
Symbolic leaf of autumn. Never seek
Your solace from the automatic hand
Of medium, or lover's partial gaze:
Truth is not found in book or litten glass
At midnight. Ghosts are liars. None may turn
Winter's hard sentence but the silly man,
The workless plowman or the unhoused poet
Who walks without a thought and finds his peace
In tall clouds mounting the unbroken wind,
In dry leaves beating at the heavens' face.

The Expected Guest

The table is spread, the lamp glitters and sighs;
Light on my eyes, light on the high curved iris
And springing from glaze to steel, from cup to knife
Makes sacramental my poor midnight table,
My broken scraps the pieces of a god.

O when they bore you down, the grinning soldiers,
Was it their white teeth you could not forget?
And when you met the beast in the myrtle wood,
When the spear broke and the blood broke out on your side
What Syrian Veronica above you
Stooped with her flaxen cloth as yet unsigned?
And either way, how could you call your darling
To drink the cup of blood your father filled?

We are dying to-night, you in the agèd darkness
And I in the white room my pride has rented.
And either way, we have to die alone.

The laid table stands hard and white as to-morrow
The lamp sings. The West wind jostles the door.
Though broken the bread, the brain, the brave body
There cannot now be any hope of changing
The leavings to living bone, the bone to bread:
For bladed centuries are drawn between us.
The room is ready, but the guest is dead.

The Wilderness

I

The red rock wilderness
Shall be my dwelling place.

Where the wind saws at the bluffs
And the pebble falls like thunder
I shall watch the clawed sun
Tear the rocks asunder.

The seven-branched cactus
Will never sweat wine:
My own bleeding feet
Shall furnish the sign.

The rock says "Endure".
The wind says "Pursue".
The sun says "I will suck your bones
And afterwards bury you".

Here where the horned skulls mark the limit
Of instinct and intransigeant desire
I beat against the rough-tongued wind
Towards the heart of fire.

So knowing my youth, which was yesterday,
And my pride which shall be gone to-morrow,
I turn my face to the sun, remembering gardens
Planted by others—Longinus, Guillaume de Lorris
And all love's gardeners, in an early May.
O sing, small ancient bird, for I am going
Into the sun's garden, the red rock desert
I have dreamt of and desired more than the lilac's promise.
The flowers of the rock shall never fall.

O speak no more of love and death
And speak no word of sorrow:
My anger's eaten up my pride
And both shall die to-morrow.

Knowing I am no lover, but destroyer,
I am content to face the destroying sun.
There shall be no more journeys, nor the anguish
Of meeting and parting, after the last great parting
From the images of dancing and the gardens
Where the brown bird chokes in its song:
Until that last great meeting among mountains
Where the metal bird sings madly from the fire.

O speak no more of ceremony,
Speak no more of fame:
My heart must seek a burning land
To bury its foolish pain.

By the dry river at the desert edge
I regret the speaking rivers I have known;
The sunlight shattered under the dark bridge
And many tongues of rivers in the past.
Rivers and gardens, singing under the willows,
The glowing moon. . . .

                      And all the poets of summer
Must lament another spirit's passing over.

O never weep for me, my love,
Or seek me in this land:
But light a candle for my luck
And bear it in your hand.

III

In this hard garden where the earth's ribs
Lie bare from her first agony, I seek
The home of the gold bird, the predatory Phœnix.
O louder than the tongue of any river
Call the red flames among the shapes of rock:
And this is my calling. . . .

                      Though my love must sit
Alone with her candle in a darkened room
Listening to music that is not present or
Turning a flower in her childish hands
And though we were a thousand miles apart . . .
This is my calling, to seek the red rock desert
And speak for all those who have lost the gardens,
Forgotten the singing, yet dare not find the desert—
To sing the song that rises from the fire.
  It is not profitable to remember
How my friends fell, my heroes turned to squalling
Puppets of history; though I would forget

The way of this one's failure, that one's exile—
How the small foreign girl
Grew crazed with her own beauty; how the poet
Talks to the wall in a deserted city;
How others danced until the Tartar wind
Blew in the doors; or sitting alone at midnight
Heard Solomon Eagle beat his drum in the streets:
This is the time to ask their pardon
For any act of coldness in the past.
There is no kind of space can separate us:
No weather, even this cruel sun, can change us;
No dress, though you in shining satin walk
Or you in velvet, while I run in tatters
Against the fiery wind. There is no loss,
Only the need to forget. This is my calling. . . .
   But behind me the rattle of stones underfoot,
Stones from the bare ridge rolling and skidding:
A voice I know, but had consigned to silence,
Another calling: my own words coming back. . . .

   "And I would follow after you
Though it were a thousand mile:
Though you crossed the deserts of the world to the kingdom of
      death, my dear,
I would follow after you and stand beside you there."

                           IV

Who is this lady, flirting with the wind,
Blown like a tangle of dried flowers through the desert?
This is my lover whom I left
Alone at evening between the candles—
White fingers nailed with flame—in an empty house.

Here we have come to the last ridge, the river
Crossed and the birds of summer left to silence.
And we go forth, we go forth together
With our lank shadows dogging us, scrambling
Across the raw red stones.
                              There is no parting
From friends, but only from the ways of friendship:
Nor from our lovers, though the forms of love
Change often as the landscape of this journey
To the dark valley where the gold bird burns.
I say, Love is a wilderness and these bones
Proclaim no failure, but the death of youth.
We say, You must be ready for the desert
Even among the orchards starred with blossom,
Even in spring, or at the waking moment
When the man turns to the woman, and both are afraid.
All who would save their life must find the desert—
The lover, the poet, the girl who dreams of Christ,
And the swift runner, crowned with another laurel:
They all must face the sun, the red rock desert,
And see the burning of the metal bird.
Until you have crossed the desert and faced that fire
Love is an evil, a shaking of the hand,
A sick pain draining courage from the heart.

We do not know the end, we cannot tell
That valley's shape, nor whether the white fire
Will blind us instantly. . . .
                              Only we go
Forward, we go forward together, leaving
Nothing except a worn-out way of loving.

V

Flesh is fire, the fire of flesh burns white
Through living limbs: a cold fire in the blood.
We must learn to live without love's food.

We shall see the sky without birds, the wind
Will blow no leaves, will ruffle no new river.
We shall walk in the desert together.
Flesh is fire, frost and fire.
We have turned in time, we shall see
The Phœnix burning under a rich tree.
Flesh is fire.

Solomon Eagle's drum shall be filled with sand:
The dancers shall wear out their skilful feet,
The pretty lady be wrapped in a rough sheet.

We go now, but others must follow:
The rivers are drying, the trees are falling,
The red rock wilderness is calling.

And they will find who linger in the garden
The way of time is not a river but
A pilferer who will not ask their pardon.

Flesh is fire, frost and fire:
Flesh is fire in this wilderness of fire
Which is our dwelling.

Printed at The Westminster Press
411a Harrow Road
London, W.9